The
Korean war:
Limits of American Power

Edited by Karl E. Valois

Soldier of the 23rd Infantry shows where his unit crossed the 38th parallel.

Discovery Enterprises, Ltd.
Carlisle, Massachusetts

© Discovery Enterprises, Ltd., Carlisle, MA 1997

ISBN 1-878668-81-1 paperback edition
Library of Congress Catalog Card Number 96-86729

10   9   8   7   6   5   4   3   2   1

Printed in the United States of America

Subject Reference Guide:

The Korean War: Limits of American Power
edited by Karl E. Valois

Korean War — U. S. History

Beginning of the Cold War — U. S. History

Acknowledgment:

The publisher and editor would like to thank
Richard and Suzanne Kobliner for their preliminary research
on primary source documents.

Photo Credits:

Cover photo: Fighting the bitter cold in Korea
was one of the battles for the troops.

Photos, courtesy of National Archives,
except where noted in the text.

Editor's notes regarding the documents:

1. *All original spelling has been retained.*

2. *A full line of dots indicates the deletion of at least an entire paragraph.*

Table of Contents

Dedication

for Mary-Ann

whose love, patience, and understanding
made this book possible

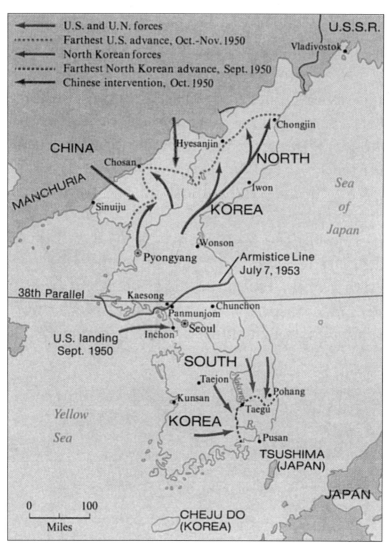

Korean War - 1950 to 1953

Introduction

by
Karl E. Valois

From 1950 to 1953, Korea, "The Land of the Morning Calm," had its tranquility profoundly disturbed. During these years, this small Asian nation served as a bloody battleground in the first major showdown of the Cold War. What began as a civil war between Korean nationalists soon escalated into a titanic military struggle between the United States and Communist China. When the guns were silenced, millions of Koreans were either killed, wounded, or homeless.

The origins of the Korean War date back to the closing days of World War II. After Japan's surrender to American and Soviet troops in 1945, the Korean peninsula, under Japanese rule since 1910, was divided at the 38th parallel by the two superpowers. By 1948, two rival regimes had been created. The Russian-sponsored People's Democratic Republic, led by Communist Kim Il Sung, assumed power in the North; Syngman Rhee, meanwhile, led the American-backed democratic, if repressive, government in the South. Both leaders vowed, however, to unify the country, and border clashes quickly erupted.

American statesmen looked upon these developments with great concern. After World War II, the administration of President Harry S. Truman believed that a sinister Communist conspiracy to conquer the world, directed from Moscow, was in progress. To block Soviet expansion, advisors such as George F. Kennan urged a new policy of "Containment." Acceptance of that idea was made official in the Truman Doctrine of 1947, by which the president announced that the United States would now assist "free peoples" resisting Communist subversion. Other policy initiatives with our Western allies — the Marshall Plan's granting of $13 billion for economic recovery.in 1948 and the creation of a mutual defense pact, NATO, one year later — also aimed at preventing the spread of Communism.

The crisis atmosphere grew even more tense with two disturbing events in 1949. First came the news in September that the Soviet Union had successfully exploded an atomic bomb, thereby ending America's nuclear monopoly. Then, in the following month, after crushing Chiang Kai-shek's Nationalist forces and forcing him into exile on the island of Formosa, Mao Tse-tung established his new Communist state, the People's Republic of China. To a stunned and bewildered American public, the overthrow of Chiang's government, which had been supported by the United States, was a staggering blow. Some Republicans, most notably Senator Joseph McCarthy, promptly charged Truman and the Democrats not only with the "loss of China" but with treason.

For a variety of reasons, therefore, when 90,000 North Korean soldiers invaded South Korea on June 25, 1950, Truman could no longer afford to be "soft on Communism." Indeed, in the president's view, the attack had been ordered by the Soviet Union. "If we let Korea down," warned Truman, "the Soviets will keep right on going and swallow up one piece of Asia after another....[Next] the Near East would collapse and no telling what would happen in Europe." As he later explained: "Communism was acting in Korea just as Hitler, Mussolini, and the Japanese had acted ten, fifteen, and twenty years earlier." This time, though, there would be no appeasement.

In characteristic fashion, Truman acted decisively. Owing to the Russian boycott of the United Nations over that body's refusal to seat Communist China, he secured a resolution from the Security Council that urged member nations to repel North Korea's aggression. Without asking Congress to declare war, he asserted his powers as Commander-in-Chief on June 27 to dispatch U.S. aircraft and warships to Korea. By early July, American soldiers had entered the conflict and seventy-year-old General Douglas MacArthur, the brilliant and legendary hero of World War II, was named Supreme U.N. Commander. While technically a U.N. "police action," the defense of South Korea, in terms of man-power, ships, planes, and supplies, was overwhelmingly an American affair. Furthermore, MacArthur received his orders from Washington.

At the outset, Americans enthusiastically applauded Truman's efforts, and one Gallup poll disclosed that 81% approved of his actions. Still, the war went badly at first. Outnumbered three-to-one and lacking equipment, American and U.N. forces could only try to slow down the North Korean advance. By September, the enemy controlled nearly all of the peninsula and had pushed U.N. troops back to the tiny Pusan perimeter. Then, in one bold stroke of genius, General MacArthur pulled off one of the greatest victories of his illustrious career.

Against the counsel of his advisors and the Joint Chiefs of Staff, MacArthur launched a daring amphibious assault on September 25 at Inchon. This port city, near the South Korean capital of Seoul, was hundreds of miles behind enemy lines. It was a dazzling triumph and, within weeks, all of South Korea had been recaptured. Elated over the news, Truman authorized MacArthur to cross the 38th parallel and push toward the Yalu River, the boundary between North Korea and China. In so doing, the president sharply redefined his goals in the hope of establishing a single "unified, independent, and democratic" Korea. On October 8, American and U.N. troops began to smash their way through North Korea.

Ominously, China had already warned that it would not "stand idly by" if its borders were endangered. Downplaying the threats, MacArthur assured Truman that the Chinese would not intervene, but if they did they would suffer "the greatest slaughter." The general badly miscalculated. On October 26, the first waves of Chinese "volunteers" furiously struck at South Korean soldiers just forty miles south of the Yalu and then, curiously, pulled back. In the meantime, with victory looming on the horizon, MacArthur still confidently predicted that "the boys will be home by Christmas." On November 24, he proceeded with his "end-the-war" offensive. Two days later, however, 300,000 Chinese troops descended upon MacArthur's unsuspecting armies and drove them all the way back below the 38th parallel in a frostbitten, demoralizing retreat.

Humiliated, MacArthur began to propose a series of provocative measures: the bombing and blockading of China, the "unleashing" of Chiang Kai-shek's forces against the Communists, the laying down of

MacArthur, left, and Truman, right, discuss the situation

radioactive wastes along the Yalu, and the dropping of 30 to 50 atomic bombs on Chinese cities. Truman rejected them all. Far from widening the conflict and perhaps triggering World War III, the president, in light of the massive Chinese intervention, now wanted peace. So, too, did the American people. A Gallup poll in January 1951 showed that 66% favored withdrawal from Korea. After General Matthew Ridgway and U.N. armies climbed back to the 38th parallel in March, Truman began to seek a cease-fire.

Sensing that he was to be deprived of his all-out war against China, MacArthur challenged the president's authority. For months he had spoken to the press, criticizing Truman's handling of the war. Now, despite warnings not to make any public policy statements, the general astonished nearly everyone. First, in open defiance of the president, on March 24, MacArthur issued his own public ultimatum to China — to make peace or be attacked in a full-scale invasion that would "doom Red China to…imminent military collapse." Next, following yet another reprimand, he wrote a letter to House Minority Leader Joseph Martin that was read aloud on the floor on April 5. In it, MacArthur denounced Truman's concept of "limited war" (confined to Korea and without atomic weapons) and the military stalemate that strategy had produced. Rather, he wrote: "There is no substitute for victory."

Privately, Truman referred to the general as "Mr. Prima Donna, Brass Hat, Five Star MacArthur," a "supreme egotist" who believed himself to be "something of a god." Yet he tolerated MacArthur's arrogance because of the latter's military genius and heroic stature. At last, however, the president had come to the conclusion that "civilian control of the military was at stake" and, as he later put it: "I didn't let it stay at stake very long." On April 11, Truman fired MacArthur. To a stunned and disbelieving public, the move was highly unpopular. One Gallup poll revealed that 69% of the American people sided with the flamboyant general (although, paradoxically, only 30% favored a war with China).

Returning to the United States for the first time since 1937, MacArthur was treated to a reception of delirious crowds and ticker-tape parades.

MacArthur was welcomed in a ticker-tape parade.

Then, on April 19, in one of the most memorable speeches ever made before a joint session of Congress, he electrified the gathering and a nationwide television audience with an emotion-packed defense of his actions. Just before he bid farewell, he uttered the famous lines: "Old soldiers never die. They just fade away." Yet within a short time, the cheering stopped. Particularly effective in quieting the uproar was General Omar Bradley's sobering comment that a full-fledged conflict with China would be "the wrong war, at the wrong place, at the wrong time, and with the wrong enemy." In the end, MacArthur was indeed allowed to "fade away."

Peace talks began at Panmunjom in July 1951. But, both at the conference table and the battlefront, an agonizing deadlock stymied progress for two years. The "meat-grinder" offensive of General Ridgway, who replaced MacArthur, inflicted heavy casualties while gaining little ground. Gone forever were the dramatic advances and pell-mell retreats.

General Matthew Ridgway (left), is seen speaking with a divisional commander. The grenade on his webbing became his personal hallmark.

Instead, savage fighting raged on for numbered hills and ridgelines — the Battle of Hill 1179, Heartbreak Ridge — near the 38th parallel. Truce negotiations became snarled over a number of issues, the most serious of which were prisoner exchanges and the stubborn objections of Syngman Rhee to any settlement that would not include the demise of North Korea's regime.

As the presidential election of 1952 drew near, the war remained mired in a bloody stalemate. When President Truman's popularity continued to sag, he announced that he would not seek another term and the Democrats nominated Adlai Stevenson. Brimming with confidence, Republicans chose Dwight David Eisenhower, the famed Allied Supreme Commander of World War II, who was easily the most popular man in America. With his last-minute pledge — "I shall go to Korea" — Eisenhower promised to end the war. On election day, voters sent the military hero to the White House in a landslide.

But once in office, Eisenhower encountered difficulties, especially the "prisoners of war" controversy. Under customary international procedure, all POWs were simply exchanged. About 85,000 Chinese and North Korean soldiers, however, did not want to return home, and several hundred American and South Korean captives (having been subject to Communist "brainwashing") preferred to live in North Korea. Like Truman earlier, Eisenhower was opposed to the return of any prisoners to Communist rule. With no breakthrough in sight, the president, unwilling to accept the status quo in Korea, informed the Chinese that he was ready for a massive escalation of the war and was prepared to use atomic weapons. At the same time, he managed to pacify Rhee with promises of future military and economic aid.

Finally, on June 27, 1953, the long-awaited armistice was signed. Reflecting the military position of both sides at the end of hostilities, the Korean boundary was set a little north of the 38th parallel, with a 2 1/2-mile-wide demilitarized zone separating the two Koreas. The troublesome POW issue was referred to a panel of neutral nations, which later ruled that each captive's choice of residence be honored (twenty-one Americans chose North Korea).

Some of the American who chose to stay in North Korea.

Though no precise figures have been attained, the "limited war" took a heavy toll in human life: 2,500,000 North Koreans, 1,100,000 South Koreans, and 1,000,000 Chinese. The war cost 54,246 American lives, with another 103,284 wounded or missing. Interestingly, though border skirmishes have continued for decades, the two Koreas, China, and the United States have scheduled talks for August 1997 that will hopefully lead to a final peace treaty.

In all, the Korean War became one of the most important events in recent history. Among the positive results for the United States was the fact that Communist aggression in Korea was repelled. To be sure, no clear-cut military victory bringing about unification was achieved, but neither did South Korea fall into enemy hands. Moreover, South Korea went on to become a major economic power in the Far East. Likewise, the war gave assurances to Japan that it could rely on American military support to protect its new democratic government. And $3 billion in U.S. war-related purchases from Japan during the fighting began to propel the Japanese economy to new heights. Lastly, while only about one-quarter of its member nations supplied troops, the United Nations proved that it would act militarily to restore peace.

Far-reaching consequences occurred in the political and diplomatic realms as well. The stalemated conflict helped to undermine the popularity of Truman and his party, place a Republican in the White House, and fan the flames of McCarthyism. Truman, meanwhile, enormously expanded presidential powers by sending forces into battle without a Congressional declaration of war. In addition, the annual defense budget skyrocketed from $13 billion in 1949 to $53 billion in 1953, and hovered around the $40 billion mark for the rest of the 1950s.

In line with this thinking, the Cold War became globalized, as the United States sought new bases and new alliances, and increased military aid to countries combatting Communism. No longer confining the Communist threat to Europe and the Middle East, American statesmen became more and more concerned with events in Southeast Asia. Indeed, it would soon be here, in the remote jungles of Vietnam, where American leaders would again fail to learn perhaps the most important lesson of the Korean War — namely, that for all its wealth, technology, and sophisticated military weaponry, there were limits to American power.

Containment

The Truman Doctrine

In a dramatic appearance before Congress on March 12, 1947, President Truman espoused a set of ideas that came to be known as the Truman Doctrine. Much of the speech dealt with his request to provide Greece and Turkey with $400 million in aid to combat alleged Soviet attempts to impose "totalitarian regimes" on both nations. Truman went on to add, however, that it was the duty of the United States to halt the spread of Communism everywhere. This "containment" policy would chart the course of American foreign relations for nearly a half-century. Here are excerpts from the address.

Source: *Public Papers of the Presidents of the United States, Harry S. Truman, 1947* (Washington, D.C.: U.S. Government Printing Office, 1963), pp. 176-180.

Mr. President, Mr. Speaker, Members of the Congress of the United States:

The gravity of the situation which confronts the world today necessitates my appearance before a joint session of the Congress.

The foreign policy and the national security of this country are involved.

....

To ensure the peaceful development of nations, free from coercion, the United States has taken a leading part in establishing the United Nations. The United Nations is designed to make possible lasting freedom and independence for all its members. We shall not realize our objectives, however, unless we are willing to help free peoples to maintain their free institutions and their national integrity against aggressive movements that seek to impose upon them totalitarian regimes. This is no more than a frank recognition that totalitarian regimes imposed upon free peoples, by direct or indirect aggression, undermine the foundations of international peace and hence the security of the United States.

....

I believe that it must be the policy of the United States to support free peoples who are resisting attempted subjugation by armed minorities or by outside pressures.

I believe that we must assist free peoples to work out their own destinies in their own way.

....

The seeds of totalitarian regimes are nurtured by misery and want. They spread and grow in the evil soil of poverty and strife. They reach their full growth when the hope of a people for a better life has died.

We must keep that hope alive.

The free peoples of the world look to us for support in maintaining their freedoms.

If we falter in our leadership, we may endanger the peace of the world-and we shall surely endanger the welfare of this Nation.

Mr. "X" - George F. Kennan

Scholar, career diplomat, and expert on the Soviet Union, George F. Kennan was one of the major architects of the Cold War. While serving as head of the State Department's Policy Planning Staff, he produced a highly influential explanation of the "containment" doctrine in a 1947 article published anonymously in Foreign Affairs. *Still, to the author's own regret later, the enigmatic Mr. "X" never precisely specified how the Soviets were to be "contained" or in what areas of the globe the doctrine should be applied. What follows are highlights from that important article.*

Source: "X," "The Sources of Soviet Conduct," *Foreign Affairs*, Volume 25 (July 1947), pp. 580-582.

It is clear that the United States cannot expect in the foreseeable future to enjoy political intimacy with the Soviet regime. It must continue to regard the Soviet Union as a rival, not a partner, in the political arena. It must continue to expect that Soviet policies will reflect no abstract love of peace and stability, no real faith in the possibility of a permanent happy coexistence of the Socialist and capitalist worlds, but rather a cautious, persistent pressure toward the disruption and weakening of all rival influence and rival power.

Balanced against this are the facts that Russia, as opposed to the western world in general, is still by far the weaker party, that Soviet policy is highly flexible, and that Soviet society may well contain deficiencies which will eventually weaken its own total potential. This would of itself warrant the United States entering with reasonable confidence upon a policy of firm containment, designed to confront the Russians with unalterable counter-force at every point where they show signs of encroaching upon the interests of a peaceful and stable world.

....

It would be an exaggeration to say that American behavior unassisted and alone could exercise a power of life and death over the communist movement and bring about the early fall of Soviet power in Russia. But the United States has it in its power to increase enormously the strains under which Soviet policy must operate, to force upon the Kremlin a far greater degree of moderation and circumspection than it has had to observe in recent years, and in this way to promote tendencies which must eventually find their outlet in either the break-up or the gradual mellowing of Soviet power.

....

Thus the decision will really fall in large measure in this country itself. The issue of Soviet-American relations is in essence a test of the over-all worth of the United States as a nation among nations. To avoid destruction the United States need only measure up to its own best traditions and prove itself worthy of preservation as a great nation.

Truman Sends Air and Naval Support

On June 27, 1950, as North Korean tanks were streaming into the South Korean capital of Seoul, President Truman held an emergency meeting with Congressional leaders to brief them on the rapidly deteriorating situation there. Using his powers as Commander-in-Chief, Truman informed them he had decided to send American air and naval support to the forces of South Korea. Minutes after the conference ended, anxious reporters were handed a presidential statement which, when read aloud in the Congress, brought a wave of cheers. Soon, the "containment" doctrine would be put to its greatest test yet. Here are portions of the press release.

Source: *Public Papers of the Presidents of the United States, Harry S. Truman, 1950* (Washington, D.C.: U.S. Government Printing Office, 1963), p. 492.

In Korea the Government forces, which were armed to prevent border raids and to preserve internal security, were attacked by invading forces from North Korea. The Security Council of the United Nations called upon the invading troops to cease hostilities and to withdraw to the 38th parallel. This they have not done, but on the contrary have pressed the attack. The Security Council called upon all members of the United Nations to render every assistance to the United Nations in the execution of this resolution. In these circumstances I have ordered United States air and sea forces to give the Korean Government troops cover and support.

The attack upon Korea makes it plain beyond all doubt that communism has passed beyond the use of subversion to conquer independent nations and will now use armed invasion and war. It has defied the orders of the Security Council of the United Nations issued to preserve international peace and security.

I know that all members of the United Nations will consider carefully the consequences of this latest aggression in Korea in defiance of the Charter of the United Nations. A return to the rule of force in international affairs would have far-reaching effects. The United States will continue to uphold the rule of law.

F-86 airplanes on flight line, getting ready for combat. (U. S. Air Force)

The Early Fighting

"Holding Action"

To forestall the imminent collapse of South Korea, Truman made what he later regarded to be the toughest decision of his presidency — the commitment of U.S. ground forces into the conflict. In July 1950, however, the first 10,000 American soldiers and their 25,000 South Korean allies could fight no more than a desperate "holding action" against North Korea's 90,000 troops. The following selection describes some of the miserable conditions of the time.

Source: *Korea—1950* (Washington, D.C.: Office of the Chief of Military History, Department of the Army, 1952), pp. 15-16.

For these men of the 24th Division, the early days of the fighting were bloody and humiliating....When they tried to retreat by road, they were subjected to a withering cross fire from the hills. Bitter, haggard, tattered, and exhausted, they withdrew [through] mud which slowed or stopped vehicular traffic and engulfed the straining leg muscles of the foot soldier. When under fire, the soldier who slipped into the stagnant, sickening waters of a rice paddy might find that only by pulling his feet out of his boots could he escape from the slime and crawl to safety. He could never escape, however, from the eternity of rain...it poured, three or four days at a time, drenching every man and coating equipment with mildew, rot or rust. The heat of the Korean summer and the inescapable flies, fleas, and lice constituted other irritants for the exasperated American troops. Nauseated by the earthy smells which thickened the air, caked with dirt, the bruised and sweat-soaked men fought the enemy

Weary soldiers of the 24th Division

in filthy, water-filled gullies, in and out of small villages of mud-plastered huts, and over endless mountain ridges... as often as not cut off from the rear, jostled by hordes of refugees, sometimes shoeless, frequently bleeding and hungry....Mingling with the civilians, enemy personnel in native dress moved inconspicuously, waiting for opportunities to stampede the crowds, block bridges, and throw hand grenades into passing groups of U.S. soldiers.

Recollections of Private Robert Harper

During the first days of the war the lack of armor-piercing shells made it extremely difficult to stop the advance of the North Koreans and their Russian-made T-34 tanks. In this account, Robert Harper, an American private, recalls the futility that resulted in the evacuation of the south Korean city of Ch'onan.

Source: Donald Knox, *The Korean War, Pusan to Chosin: An Oral History* (New York: Harcourt, Brace, Jovanovich, 1985), pp. 37-39.

We heard all kinds of fighting going on up north but didn't really know what was happening. Soon our platoon sergeant came around [7 July], took every available man not essential to regimental headquarters, loaded us in trucks and jeeps and told us we were going up to Ch'onan. We would try to hold the position there as long as possible.

....

During the day I talked to some of the officers and men who'd been fighting farther north. One officer told me the biggest problem was in not being able to stop the Russian T34 tanks. Our bazookas were too small and firing one of them at a tank was the same as throwing a rock at it; the shells just bounced off the armor. He said we had to somehow try to stop the tanks because that would also slow down their infantry....

....

The sun went down. It was a long, long night; quiet, no firing. If you had to move, you moved in the dark real slow and tried to make no noise. As daylight broke [8 July], we heard this loud clanking noise off the the [sic] left. We understood now what was happening — their tanks were coming....We had no way of stopping them. They came to the end of the road and I could hear them firing. I did not know which of our companies were down there but knew they were catching hell. We were ordered back to a narrow street, where we waited to see what would happen next....

Wounded soldier being brought down from the hills.

We ran down through some alleys and met some more GIs who said orders had been issued to evacuate the town. I could hear a lot of small-arms and mortar fire behind me. We went to the east edge of town, worked our way through rice paddies and got to the road. There were quite a few civilians still on the road. We joined them in heading south. We drew heavy artillery fire and began to lose a lot of people.

The Tide Turns

Forces Land at Inchon

With one bold stroke of genius on September 15, 1950, General Douglas MacArthur put an end to the demoralizing retreats of the preceding months. Overcoming obstacles (including treacherous tides of at least 30 feet), an invasion force of 262 ships and 70,000 troops successfully landed at the port of Inchon, some 200 miles northwest of Pusan. Within weeks, United Nations forces had reached the 38th parallel and were in firm control of South Korea. A chronicle of the "miracle" at Inchon appeared in Time.

Source: *Time*, September 25, 1950, pp. 25-30.

Massive U.N. air strikes softened Inchon's beaches and all land approaches to the port. As Admiral James H. Doyle's task force approached, six destroyers gamely plowed ahead, drew and silenced the fire of hidden enemy batteries on Wolmi island. Several ships were damaged, one severely. Then the U.S. 1st Marine Division hit the beaches.

....

On landing day last week, in the dawn's early light, MacArthur picked his way through a confusion of men in helmets and life jackets, climbed onto the admiral's bridge chair. He wore his old braided, sweat-stained garrison cap.

....

Then the naval bombardment began, and he raised his glasses to watch. The planes came. We could see the streaks of their rockets, and minutes later hear the booms. General Almond, the new X Corps commander, came up. "Good morning, General," he said. "How are you?" "I don't see how I could be better," answered MacArthur.

When the ship's speaker announced: "The first wave of the attack force is ashore," MacArthur nodded to Doyle. Then the speaker called: "All boats are ashore from the first and second waves. The troops are fanning out rapidly. No casualties so far." MacArthur lowered his head a little, and then a broad grin spread across his face. The night before, he had said we would not take more than 100 casualties on the morning objectives. Now all waves were ashore, with only 15 casualties reported.

As U.S. soldiers walk to battle, civilian refugees flee.

Early next morning, with Marine tanks alongside, Easy Company moved through the remainder of Inchon. Civilians were moving back into the town they had fled the day before. We met them along the road which skirts the city's southern flank. They lined the streets and intersections, cheered and clapped their hands. Marine veterans, who started out with rifles at high port, eyes scanning the buildings ahead and watching for mines, became a bit flustered at this demonstration of public affection. Soon they brought their rifles down from the ready and slung them over their shoulders.

MacArthur's "End-the-War" Drive

By October 1950, MacArthur was directed by Truman to cross the 38th parallel and to push to the Yalu River, the boundary between North Korea and China. Over the next few weeks, U.N. armies nearly conquered all of North Korea. Although Chinese soldiers crossed the river to attack the "invaders," they quickly pulled back. Unfettered, MacArthur launched his "end-the-war" drive on November 24. The optimism of the moment was captured in a Time *article.*

Source: *Time*, December 4, 1950, p. 22.

On the first day of the new Allied drive for the Yalu, Douglas MacArthur issued a confident communiqué: "The United Nations massive compression envelopment in North Korea against the new Red armies operating there is now approaching its decisive effort....If successful, this should for all practical purposes end the war, restore peace and unity to Korea, enable the prompt withdrawal of United Nations military forces, and permit the complete assumption by [Korea] of full sovereignty and international equality. It is that for which we fight."

The occasion seemed important enough to merit another MacArthur visit to the front....

....

To the 24th Division's Major General John Church MacArthur said that he was recommending the 24th for a presidential citation, and added: "I have already promised wives and mothers that the boys of the 24th Division will be back by Christmas. Don't make me a liar. Get to the Yalu and I will relieve you."

The Threat of China

1st Marine Division captures Chinese communists on the central Korean front. (Marine Corps)

"Hate America" Campaign

In 1949, Mao Tse-tung's Communist rebels seized power in China by over-throwing the American-backed government of Chiang Kai-shek and forcing Chiang and his army into exile on the island of Formosa. There, the United States continued to offer him protection and support. One year later, the Red Chinese inaugurated a vicious "Hate America" campaign via organized rallies and newspaper editorials. Here are some examples.

Source: Robert Leckie, *Conflict: The History of the Korean War* (New York: DaCapo Press, 1996), p. 158.

This mad dog [the U.S.] seizes Formosa between its hind legs while with its teeth it violently bites the Korean people. Now one of its forelegs has been poked into our Northeast front. Its bloodswollen eyes cast around for something fur-ther to attack. All the world is under its threat. The American imperialist mad dog is half beaten up. Before it dies, it will go on biting and tearing.

The [U.S.] is the paradise of gangsters, swindlers, rascals, special agents, fascist germs, speculators, debauchers, and all the dregs of mankind. This is the world's manufactory and source of such crimes as reaction, darkness, cruelty, decadence, corruption, debauchery, oppression of man by man, and cannibalism. This is the exhibition ground of all the crimes which can possibly be committed by mankind. This is a living hell, ten times, one hundred times, one thousand times worse than can possibly be depicted by the most sanguinary of writers. Here the criminal phenomena that issue forth defy the imagination of human brains. Conscientious persons can only wonder how the spiritual civilization of mankind can be depraved to such an extent.

Another scathing indictment of the United States came on September 23, 1950 in the People's Daily, *the largest and most influential newspaper in Red China. In this selection, the Chinese Communists provided a litany of American "misdeeds" that would justify China's support for North Korea.*

Source: Robert Leckie, *op. cit.*, p. 159.

We Chinese people are against the American imperialists because they are against us. They have openly become the archenemy of the People's Republic of China by supporting the people's enemy, the Chiang Kai-shek clique, by sending a huge fleet to prevent the liberation of the Chinese territory of Formosa, by repeated air intrusions and strafing and bombing of the Chinese people, by refusing new China a seat in the UN, through intrigues with their satellite nations, by rearing up again a fascist power in Japan, and by rearming Japan for the purpose of expanding aggressive war. Is it not just for us to support our friend and neighbor against our enemy? The American warmongers are mistaken in thinking that their accusations and threats will intimidate the people of China.

Truman Poses "The" Question

The possibility of Chinese intervention loomed large in Truman's think-ing. When the president flew to Wake Island on October 15, 1950 to meet MacArthur for the first and only time, the general greeted him with good news: "I believe that formal resistance will end throughout North and South Korea by Thanksgiving." Then, Truman posed his now-famous question.

Source: *Foreign Relations of the United States, 1950*, Volume 7 (Washington, D.C.: U.S. Government Printing Office, 1976), pp. 949, 953-954.

The President: What are the chances for Chinese or Soviet interference?

General MacArthur: Very little. Had they interfered in the first or second months it would have been decisive. We are no longer fearful of their intervention. We no longer stand hat in hand. The Chinese have 300,000 men in Manchuria. Of these probably not more than 100/125,000 are distrib-uted along the Yalu River. Only 50/60,000 could be gotten across the Yalu River. They have no Air Force. Now that we have bases for our Air Force in Korea, if the Chinese tried to get down to Pyongyang there would be the greatest slaughter.

With the Russians it is a little different. They have an Air Force in Siberia and a fairly good one, with excellent pilots equipped with some jets and B-25 and B-29 planes. They can put 1,000 planes in the air with some 2/300 more from the Fifth and Seventh Soviet Fleets. They are probably no match for our Air Force. The Russians have no ground troops available for North Korea. They would have diffi-culty in putting troops into the field. It would take six weeks to get a division across and six weeks brings the winter. The only other combination would be Russian air support of Chinese ground troops. Russian air is deployed in a semi-circle through Mukden and Harbin, but the coordination between the Russian air and the Chinese ground would be

UN artillery

so flimsy that I believe Russian air would bomb the Chinese as often as they would bomb us. Ground support is a very difficult thing to do. Our Marines do it perfectly. They have been trained for it. Our own Air and Ground Forces are not as good as the Marines but they are effective. Between untrained Air and Ground Forces an air umbrella is impossible without a lot of joint training. I believe it just wouldn't work with Chinese Communist ground and Russian air. We are the best.

Retreat

No Time for Optimism

Contrary to MacArthur's expectations, the Chinese did intervene. Entering North Korea on October 26, 1950, the first wave of Chinese soldiers fiercely engaged South Korean troops just forty miles south of the Yalu River. As MacArthur went on to say, now it had become "a new war." The selection that follows, a letter from Captain Norman Allen, describes the changed situation.

Source: Donald Knox, *The Korean War, Pusan to Chosin: An Oral History* (New York: Harcourt, Brace, Jovanovich, 1985), pp. 439-440.

4 Nov

Dearest Mother:

Today is cold. Rain last night and this morning, cold wind and really mean.

Our regiment yesterday moved 56 miles back SE to Sunch'on. I watched civilians moving out; women carrying what they could on their heads, kids strapped to their backs, those a little older walking alongside or running to keep up.

....

It's a nasty realization with the casualties returning on jeeps and tanks, that the war is still on and we are still in it. We see issues of *Time* and *Newsweek* stating, "War over — only mopping up — troops in Japan for Thanksgiving — home by Christmas." Wish the people who write this were over here now. This is certainly no time for optimism.

American and South Korean soldiers (Imperial War Museum)

In another letter one month later, Captain Allen continued to vent his frustrations. Moreover, the entrance into the war of 300,000 Chinese troops in late November added to an even greater sense of urgency. Here are some of his thoughts.

Source: Donald Knox, *op. cit.*, pp. 651-652.

---

2 December — Sunch'on

Mother darling:

....

...We ought to be able to get together somehow — instead of fighting. Trying to fight, with all the strategic angles completely tied up in politics is impossible. The UN ought to withdraw to the 38th [Parallel]....We were originally committed to protect the democratic rights of a small nation from armed Communist aggression. We accomplished this when we hit the 38th Parallel in October. I can see where we had to eliminate the threat of the [North Koreans] doing it all over again. But the Chinese intervention has changed the whole picture. It's almost a case of saving what we can unless the politicos can arrive at some compromise, and soon.

....

...[T]hey ought to bring the UN conferees over here, put them in this cold, give them insufficient food, no smokes, let them get dirty and tired. Tell them then, "Now you all just sit here until you get things settled."

MacArthur Overestimated

Surveying the wreckage brought on by the intervention of massive Chinese armies, Time *offered the following assessment of MacArthur's efforts.*

Source: *Time*, December 11, 1950, p. 26.

In North Korea, he tried what he called a "massive compression envelopment" against greatly superior forces. He undoubtedly underestimated the size and the quality of the Chinese troops. Their lack of tanks, artillery and transport looked like fatal weakness to exponents of current U.S. military doctrines. Specifically, MacArthur overestimated the effect of his air power on the Chinese troops.

The enveloped Chinese broke through the envelopment. Their thrust was so wide, deep, and strong that his inadequate reserves (grouped around the 1st Cavalry Division) could not check it. MacArthur's center was gone and the Reds lapped around the two inside flanks of his divided army, pushing both wings back toward the sea.

Morale Shaken

Shortly before Christmas, 1950, Time's *coverage of the war included this interesting interpretation of events.*

Source: *Time*, December 18, 1950, p. 25.

The best to be said of Korea was that the worst had not happened. The U.S. forces threatened with annihilation a fortnight ago had not been destroyed, and were not likely to be destroyed. Lieut. General Walton H. Walker's rapid withdrawal of the Eighth Army saved most of it; the fighting retreat of the X Corps in the northeast saved most of that command, too.

Despite uncountable acts of individual and group heroism, the morale of the surviving U.S. troops had been severely shaken by the knowledge that all their shiny weapons and equipment, their sensational blitz tactics, their mountain of supplies, their tanks, trucks, artillery and air power could not hold back a horde that moved on foot, without air support, without armor and with hardly any weapon larger than a mortar. The American fighting man had moved a long way from the revolutionary rabble of 1775; he had become, in a manner of speaking, the British Redcoat of 1950 — confident of superiority and aware of the power of a great nation behind him, but unable to cope with ragged characters firing from ambush.

Truman vs. MacArthur

"With deep regret..."

UN helicopter makes a forced landing in a farmer's field.

After Chinese forces sent U.N. troops on a full-scale retreat, MacArthur, as we have seen, urged provocative new measures against China and openly criticized Truman's leadership. Repeated warnings from the president were ignored until, finally, on April 11, 1951, Truman fired the legendary general. Here is the president's written statement that was submitted to a stunned White House press corp.

Source: *Public Papers of the Presidents of the United States, Harry S. Truman, 1951* (Washington, D.C.: U.S. Government Printing Office, 1965), p. 222.

With deep regret I have concluded that General of the Army Douglas MacArthur is unable to give his wholehearted support to the policies of the United States Government and of the United Nations in matters pertaining to his official duties. In view of the specific responsibilities imposed upon me by the Constitution of the United States and the added responsibility which has been entrusted to me by the United Nations, I have decided that I must make a change of command in the Far East. I have, therefore, relieved General MacArthur of his commands and have designated Lt. Gen. Matthew B. Ridgway as his successor.

Full and vigorous debate on matters of national policy is a vital element in the constitutional system of our free democracy. It is fundamental, however, that military commanders must be governed by the policies and directives issued to them in the manner provided by our laws and Constitution. In time of crisis, this consideration is particularly compelling.

General MacArthur's place in history as one of our greatest commanders is fully established. The Nation owes him a debt of gratitude for the distinguished and exceptional service which he has rendered his country in posts of great responsibility. For that reason I repeat my regret at the necessity for the action I feel compelled to take in his case.

Preventing a Third World War

The dismissal of General MacArthur sent shock waves across the land. In a live radio broadcast to the nation later that evening, President Truman defended his controversial action by explaining his war aims in Korea. The following excerpts are from that historic address.

Source: *ibid.,* pp. 223-227.

My fellow Americans:

I want to talk to you plainly tonight about what we are doing in Korea and about our policy in the Far East.

In the simplest terms, what we are doing in Korea is this: We are trying to prevent a third world war.

....

It is right for us to be in Korea now. It was right last June. It is right today.

I want to remind you why this is true.

The Communists in the Kremlin are engaged in a monstrous conspiracy to stamp out freedom all over the world. If they were to succeed, the United States would be numbered among their principal victims. It must be clear to everyone that the United States cannot — and will not — sit idly by and await foreign conquest.

....

The aggression against Korea is the boldest and most dangerous move the Communists have yet made.

The attack on Korea was part of a greater plan for conquering all of Asia.

....

The whole Communist imperialism is back of the attack on peace in the Far East. It was the Soviet Union that trained and equipped the North Koreans for aggression. The Chinese Communists massed 44 well-trained and well-equipped divisions on the Korean frontier. These were the troops they threw into battle when the North Korean Communists were beaten.

....

So far, by fighting a limited war in Korea, we have prevented aggression from succeeding, and bringing on a general war. And the ability of the whole free world to resist Communist aggression has been greatly improved.

....

We do not want to see the conflict in Korea extended. We are trying to prevent a world war — not to start one. And the best way to do that is to make it plain that we and the other free countries will continue to resist the attack.

But you may ask why can't we take other steps to punish the aggressor. Why don't we bomb Manchuria and China itself? Why don't we assist the Chinese Nationalist troops to land on the mainland of China?

If we were to do these things we would be running a very grave risk of starting a general war. If that were to happen, we would have brought about the exact situation we are trying to prevent.

....

The dangers are great. Make no mistake about it. Behind the North Koreans and Chinese Communists in the front lines stand additional millions of Chinese soldiers. And behind the Chinese stand the tanks, the planes, the submarines, the soldiers, and the scheming rulers of the Soviet Union.

....

I believe that we must try to limit the war to Korea for these vital reasons: to make sure that the precious lives of our fighting men are not wasted; to see that the security of our country and the free world is not needlessly jeopardized; and to prevent a third world war.

A number of events have made it evident that General MacArthur did not agree with that policy. I have therefore considered it essential to relieve General MacArthur so that there would be no doubt or confusion as to the real purpose and aim of our policy.

It was with deepest personal regret that I found myself compelled to take this action. General MacArthur is one of our greatest military commanders. But the cause of world peace is much more important than any individual.

....

The struggle of the United Nations in Korea is a struggle for peace.

Free nations have united their strength in an effort to prevent a third world war.

That war can come if the Communist rulers want it to come. But this Nation and its allies will not be responsible for its coming.

We do not want to widen the conflict. We will use every effort to prevent that disaster. And in so doing, we know that we are following the great principles of peace, freedom, and justice.

General MacArthur Addresses Congress

Upon his return to the United States, MacArthur accepted an invitation to speak before the Congress on April 19, 1951. There, in one of the most remarkable scenes in American history, the fallen general presented his side of the story. With a record television audience of thirty million and millions more listening on radio, he delivered an impassioned defense of his policies. Shrewdly, however, he did not specifically mention his desire to use atomic weapons against China. And although his oration was interrupted numerous times by thunderous applause and wild cheering, few Congressmen were willing to implement his proposals. Here are portions of the speech.

Source: *Congressional Record*, Volume 97 (April 19,1951), pp. 4123-45.

I do not stand here as advocate for any partisan cause, for the issues are fundamental and reach quite beyond the realm of partisan consideration. They must be resolved on the highest plane of national interest if our course is to prove sound and our future protected. I trust, therefore, that you will do me the justice of receiving that which I have to say as solely expressing the considered viewpoint of a fellow American. I address you with neither rancor nor bitterness in the fading twilight of life with but one purpose in mind-to serve my country. [Applause.]

...While I was not consulted prior to the President's decision to intervene in support of the Republic of Korea, that decision, from a military standpoint, proved a sound one [applause] as we hurled back the invaders and decimated his forces. Our victory was complete and our objectives within reach when Red China intervened with numerically superior ground forces. This created a new war and an entirely new situation — a situation not contemplated when our forces were committed against the North Korean invaders — a situation which called for new decisions in the diplomatic sphere to permit the realistic adjustment of military strategy. Such decisions have not been forthcoming. [Applause.]

While no man in his right mind would advocate sending our ground forces into continental China and such was never given a thought, the new situation did urgently demand a drastic revision of strategic planning if our political aim was to defeat this new enemy as we had defeated the old. [Applause.]

Apart from the military need as I saw it to neutralize the sanctuary protection given the enemy north of the Yalu, I felt that military necessity in the conduct of the war made mandatory:

1. The intensification of our economic blockade against China;

2. The imposition of a naval blockade against the China coast;

3. Removal of restrictions on air reconnaissance of China's coast areas and of Manchuria [applause];

4. Removal of restrictions on the forces of the Republic of China on Formosa with logistical support to contribute to their effective operations against the common enemy. [Applause.]

For entertaining these views, all professionally designed to support our forces committed to Korea and bring hostilities to an end with the least possible delay and at a saving of countless American and Allied lives, I have been severely criticized in lay circles, principally abroad, despite my understanding that from a military standpoint the above views have been fully shared in the past by practically every military leader concerned with the Korea campaign, including our own Joint Chiefs of Staff. [Applause, the Members rising.]

...We could hold in Korea by constant maneuver and at an approximate area where our supply line advantages were in balance with the supply line disadvantages of the enemy, but we could hope at best for only an indecisive campaign, with its terrible and constant attrition upon our forces if the enemy utilized his full military potential. I have constantly called for the new political decisions essential to a solution. Efforts have been made to distort my position. It has been said, in effect, that I am a warmonger. Nothing could be further from the truth. I know war as few other men now living know it, and nothing to me is more revolting. I have long advocated its complete abolition as its very destructiveness on both friend and foe has rendered it useless as a means of settling international disputes.

But once war is forced upon us, there is no other alternative than to apply every available means to bring it to a swift end. War's very object is victory — not prolonged indecision. [Applause.] In war, indeed, there can be no substitute for victory. [Applause.] There are some who for varying reasons would appease Red China. They are blind to history's clear lesson. For history teaches with unmistakable emphasis that appeasement but begets new and bloodier war....Why, my soldiers asked of me, surrender military advantages to an enemy in the field? I could not answer. [Applause.] Some may say to avoid spread of the conflict into an all-out war with China; others, to avoid Soviet intervention.

....

I have just left your fighting sons in Korea. They have met all tests there and I can report to you without reservation they are splendid in every way. [Applause.] It was my constant effort to preserve them and end this savage conflict honorably and with the least loss of time and a minimum sacrifice of life. Its growing bloodshed has caused me the deepest anguish and anxiety. Those gallant men will remain often in my thoughts and in my prayers always. [Applause.]

I am closing my 52 years of military service. [Applause.] When I joined the Army even before the turn of the century, it was the fulfillment of all my boyish hopes and dreams. The world has turned over many times since I took the oath on the plain at West Point, and the hopes and dreams have long since vanished. But I still remember the refrain of one of the most popular barrack ballads of that day which proclaimed most proudly that —

"Old soldiers never die; they just fade away."

And like the old soldier of that ballad, I now close my military career and just fade away — an old soldier who tried to do his duty as God gave him the light to see that duty.

Good-by.

McCarthyism

Of all the criticism of Truman's handling of the war, perhaps none surpassed in notoriety and venom that of Joseph McCarthy. From 1950 to 1954, the Republican senator from Wisconsin became one of the most powerful and feared leaders in Washington. Yet his crusade to uncover a sinister Communist conspiracy to overthrow American democracy — filled with lies, deceit, and false accusations failed to identify a single Communist and instead earned him disgrace and censure. Here, in the Senate chamber on April 24, 1951, McCarthy mounted a sensational attack on Truman and Secretary of State Dean Acheson.

Source: *Congressional Record*, Volume 97 (April 24, 1951), pp. 4253, 4261.

Mr. McCarthy....[T]here is one fact which stands out and which no one can successfully contradict, namely, that so long as we tie the hands of General Stratemeyer and our other generals in that theater, so long as we tell them they cannot fight back, so long as we let Chinese Communist planes come over and kill our American boys[,]...so long as we follow that type of reasoning, more American boys will die than would die if we followed General MacArthur's advice and destroyed their planes.

....

In connection with the argument that we should not fight China and should not allow our men to protect themselves, because, if we do, the Russians may intervene,...then we should realize once and for all that when the time comes...that this Nation is too cowardly to fight, and is going to whine and whimper and not protect its soldiers, then this country certainly deserves no longer to exist as a nation.

McCarthy, pointing the finger

....

...It is extremely interesting, when we realize that Truman is the President of this country in name only, that the real President who discharged MacArthur is a rather sinister monster of many heads and many tentacles, a monster conceived in the Kremlin, and then given birth to by Acheson....

....

...But it is of interest to us when we realize that not Mr. Truman but Mr. Acheson,...and with the aid of the Kremlin, have succeeded in sacking one of the greatest Americans I think that was ever born, and one of the greatest military leaders since long before the days of Genghis Khan.

Stalemate

"we've been let down..."

After the Chinese Communists had driven U.N. forces all the way back into South Korea, the conflict entered a brief stage of "large-scale seesaw attacks." Finally, by the late spring of 1951, battle lines stabilized just north of the 38th parallel. Though peace talks began at Panmunjom in July, the war dragged on for another two years as a bloody military stalemate. The following letter, written by Private First Class James Cardinal, reflected the sentiments of many other American soldiers.

Source: Max Hastings, *The Korean War* (New York: Simon and Schuster, 1987), p. 176.

Dear Folks,…We are now about 60 miles NW of Taegu, holding a mountain pass thru which the entire 8th Army is moving headed south. It looks like the beginning of the end. The Chinese are kicking hell out of the U.S. Army, and I think we are getting out, at least I hope so. I think they are going to evacuate all UN troops from Korea soon, as it's impossible to stop these Chinese hordes. Theres [sic] just too many of them for us to fight in Korea. If the big wheels in Washington decide to fight here it will be the biggest mistake they ever made, as I don't think we can hold the [Chinese]. Anyway, lets [sic] hope they decide to evacuate us.

When you get complaining…letters from me, remember every soldier over here feels that way. The troops over here are mad, mad at America, Americans and America's leaders. We all feel we've been let down, by our incompetent blundering leadership, from the White House down. It seems to me to be — to hell with the troops in Korea. If we must fight communism, let's do it in Europe which is the cradle of western culture and our own civilization. It seems to me that's more worth fighting for than some barren oriental wasteland, with uncountable hordes of savage warriors. It's about time that all of you back home awakened to the truth of the matter, and let your voices be heard thru letters to your congressmen. That's the only way to get direct action. Well, folks, that's all for now. I'm in the best of health and spirits and hope that you all and the rest of the family are too. Love, Jimmy.

"I shall go to Korea..."

As the presidential election of 1952 approached, the Korean War remained a stalemated bloodbath. When President Truman (whose public approval rating had sunk to 23%) declined to seek re-election, Democrats turned to Adlai Stevenson. The Republicans, meanwhile, jubilantly nominated one of the greatest military leaders of World War II and certainly the most popular American of his era — Dwight David Eisenhower. In a move on October 24 that sealed his landslide victory, "Ike," as he was popularly known, pledged to end the war, using the memorable phrase: "I shall go to Korea." Here are some highlights of that nationally televised speech.

Source: *Text of the Address by Dwight D. Eisenhower, Republican Nominee for President, Delivered at Detroit, Michigan, October 24, 1952.* Dwight David Eisenhower Library, Abilene, Texas.

Eisenhower Campaign Train. For release in the morning papers of Saturday, October 25, 1952. Text of the Address by Dwight D. Eisenhower, Republican Nominee for President, delivered at Detroit, Michigan, October 24, 1952.

In this anxious autumn for America, one fact looms above all others in our people's mind. One tragedy challenges all men dedicated to the work of peace. One word shouts denial to those who foolishly pretend that ours is not a nation at war.

This fact, this tragedy, this word is: Korea.

....

Tonight I am going to talk about our foreign policy and of its supreme symbol — the Korean War. I am not going to give you elaborate generalizations — but hard, tough facts. I am going to state the unvarnished truth.

....

There is a Korean War — and we are fighting it — for the simplest of reasons: because free leadership failed to check and to turn back Communist ambition before it savagely attacked us. The Korean War — more perhaps than any other war in history — simply and swiftly followed the collapse of our political defenses. There is no other reason than this: we failed to read and to outwit the totalitarian mind.

....

The first task of a new administration will be to review and re-examine every course of action open to us with one goal in view: to bring the Korean War to an early and honorable end. That is my pledge to the American people.

For this task a wholly new administration is necessary. The reason for this is simple. The old administration cannot be expected to repair what it failed to prevent.

Where will a new administration begin?

It will begin with its President taking a simple, firm resolution. That resolution will be: to forego the diversions of politics and to concentrate on the job of ending the Korea War — until that job is honorably done.

That job requires a personal trip to Korea.

I shall make that trip. Only in that way could I learn how best to serve the American people in the cause of peace.

I shall go to Korea.

That is my second pledge to the American people.

Ike promised to go to Korea, and he did. (Eisenhower Library)

Carefully, then, this new administration, unfettered by past decisions and inherited mistakes, can review every factor — military, political and psychological — to be mobilized in speeding a just peace.

Progress along at least two lines can instantly begin. We can — first — step up the program of training and arming the South Korean forces. Manifestly, under the circumstances of today, United Nations forces cannot abandon that unhappy land. But just as troops of the Republic of Korea covet and deserve the honor of defending their frontiers, so should we give them maximum assistance to insure their ability to do so. Then, United Nations forces in reserve positions and supporting roles would be assurance that disaster would not again strike.

We can — secondly — shape our psychological warfare program into a weapon capable of cracking the Communist front.

Beyond all this we must carefully weigh all interrelated courses of action. We will, of course, constantly confer with associated free nations of Asia and with the cooperating members of the United Nations. Thus we could bring into being a practical plan for world peace.

That is my third pledge to you.

As the next administration goes to work for peace, we must be guided at every instant by that lesson I spoke of earlier. The vital lesson is this: to vacillate, to appease, to placate is only to invite war — vaster war — bloodier war....

I will always reject appeasement.

And that is my fourth pledge to you.

A nation's foreign policy is a much graver matter than rustling papers and bustling conferences. It is much more than diplomatic decisions and trade treaties and military arrangements.

A foreign policy is the face and the voice of a whole people. It is all that the world sees and hears and understands about a single nation. It expresses the character and the faith and the will of that nation. In this, a nation is like any individual of our personal acquaintance; the simplest gesture can betray hesitation or weakness, the merest inflection of voice can reveal doubt or fear.

It is in this deep sense that our foreign policy has faltered and failed.

....

In the great trial of this election, the judges — the people — must not be deceived into believing that the choice is between isolationism and internationalism. That is a debate of the dead past. The vast majority of Americans of both parties know that to keep their own nation free, they bear a majestic responsibility for freedom through all the world. As practical people, Americans also know the critical necessity of unimpaired access to raw materials on other continents for our own economic and military strength.

Today the choice — the real choice — lies between policies that assume that responsibility awkwardly and fearfully — and policies that accept that responsibility with sure purpose and firm will. The choice is between foresight and blindness, between doing and apologizing, between planning and improvising.

In rendering their verdict, the people must judge with courage and with wisdom. For — at this date — any faltering in America's leadership is a capital offense against freedom.

In this trial, my testimony, of a personal kind, is quite simple. A soldier all my life, I have enlisted in the greatest cause of my life — the cause of peace.

I do not believe it a presumption for me to call the effort of all who have enlisted with me — a crusade.

I use that word only to signify two facts. First: we are united and devoted to a just cause of the purest meaning to all humankind. Second: we know that — for all the might of our effort — victory can come only with the gift of God's help.

In this spirit — humble servants of a proud ideal — we do soberly say: This is a crusade.

Peace

Once elected, Eisenhower did fulfill his campaign promise to visit Korea and terminate the war. Assisted by John Foster Dulles, his Secretary of State, a truce was signed on July 27, 1953. A fascinating behind-the-scenes chronicle of events was provided by Eisenhower himself in his memoirs. What follows is a portion of that account.

A victorious Eisenhower and his wife, Mamie.

Source: Dwight D. Eisenhower, *The White House Years: Mandate for Change, 1953-1956* (Garden City, N.Y.: Doubleday and Co., 1963), pp. 178-181, 190-191.

But now, in the spring of 1953, I was President and I considered several possible lines of action. First of all would be to let the war drag on, without a change in policy. If a satisfactory armistice could not be quickly achieved, continuing this way seemed to me intolerable. We were sustaining heavy casualties for little, if any, gain.

Another plan might be to attack to the north to gain an all-out military victory by conventional means. This was the least attractive of all plans. The Chinese and North Korean Communists had sat on the same defensive line for a solid year and a half. Being diligent workers, they had done a remarkable job of digging interlaced and underground entrenchments across the entire peninsula, with positions organized in depth. They had partially overcome former logistical deficiencies by bringing in large quantities of artillery and stores of ammunition during quiet periods, and had a force in Korea superior in numbers to that of the ROK and United Nations forces combined.

These facts would not in themselves necessarily preclude an attack. The UN enjoyed air superiority, and, with the superior weapons and equipment and highly developed logistical system of the UN forces, an attack might well have been successful, particularly if accompanied by an amphibious landing in the enemy's rear. Nevertheless, any such attack would be costly, whether the objective was local or unlimited. The big tactical problem would be the breakthrough of the defense positions. Moreover, if the purpose were to occupy the major part of the peninsula of Korea, success would put us in an extremely awkward position, with a substantial occupation of territory but no ability to use our weapons to complete the victory — that is, unless the "sanctuary" concept were discarded and attack on airfields and targets in Manchuria were allowed. Such a change would increase the danger of spreading the war.

....

Clearly, then, a course of action other than a conventional ground attack in Korea was necessary.

In the light of my unwillingness to accept the status quo, several other moves were considered in the event that the Chinese Communists refused to accede to an armistice in a reasonable time. These possibilities differed in detail, but in order to back up any of them, we had to face several facts.

First, it was obvious that if we were to go over to a major offensive, the war would have to be expended outside of Korea — with strikes against the supporting Chinese airfields in Manchuria, a blockade of the Chinese coast, and similar measures. Second, a build-up of both United States and [South Korean] forces would be necessary....

Finally, to keep the attack from becoming overly costly, it was clear that we would have to use atomic weapons.

....

If we decided upon a major, new type of offensive, the present policies would have to be changed and the new ones agreed to by our allies. Foremost would be the proposed use of atomic weapons....My feeling was then, and still remains, that it would be impossible for the United States to maintain the military commitments which it now sustains around the world (without turning into a garrison state) did we not possess atomic weapons and the will to use them when necessary. But an American decision to use them at that time would have created strong disrupting feelings between ourselves and our allies. However, if an all-out offensive should be highly successful, I felt that the rifts so caused could, in time, be repaired.

Of course, there were other problems, not the least of which would be the possibility of the Soviet Union entering the war. In nuclear warfare the Chinese Communists would have been able to do little. But we knew that the

Soviets had atomic weapons in quantity and estimated that they would soon explode a hydrogen device....

....

The lack of progress in the long-stalemated talks — they were then recessed — and the nearly stalemated war both demanded, in my opinion, definite measures on our part to put an end to these intolerable conditions. One possibility was to let the Communist authorities understand that, in the absence of satisfactory progress, we intended to move decisively without inhibition in our use of weapons, and would no longer be responsible for confining hostilities to the Korea Peninsula. We would not be limited by any world-wide gentleman's agreement. In India and in the Formosa Straits area, and at the truce negotiations at Panmunjom, we dropped the word, discreetly, of our intention. We felt quite sure it would reach Soviet and Chinese Communist ears.

....

By...mid-July, it became apparent that a truce would probably be signed in the near future. In a White House meeting on July 23 our discussion hinged around the possible desirability of reinforcing UN units in South Korea, since a truce would mean that no more troops could be brought in on either side. Knowing this, I promptly authorized the movement to Korea of some United States units, including the 24th Infantry Division and the 1st Cavalry Division then in Japan, plus the 3rd Marine Division, located in the United States. I felt that no publicity was necessary, since there was no intent or possibility of concealing the move from the Chinese Communists.

In spite of seemingly favorable progress toward an armistice, I soon found myself writing a memorandum in near exasperation about our uncertain situation with respect to the South Korean government and the effects of this lack of close coordination on the struggle against the Communists. Our nation and the United Nations went into Korea for one reason only, to repel aggression and restore the borders of the Republic of Korea — not to reunite Korea by force. An armistice therefore would presumably mark the beginning of political discussions which would hope to reunite Korea and accomplish evacuation of the country by all troops — Chinese and United Nations'. But I had to add, "There has been so much backing and filling, indecision, doubt and frustration engendered by both Rhee and the Communists that I am doubtful that an armistice even if achieved will have any great meaning."

Fortunately I was wrong. The truce was signed three days later, on July 27, 1953.

....

As Foster Dulles and I sat and talked it over, we viewed the outcome with a measure of satisfaction. Yet this was tempered by the haunting doubt that any peaceful negotiation could reunite until the basic conflict between the Free World and Communism would one day be resolved. Soon Foster would travel to South Korea to talk with Dr. Rhee and to make preliminary arrangements to help in rehabilitating that unhappy country. Our tasks would be tedious and difficult, but they would stand in heartening contrast to what had gone before. Three years of heroism, frustration, and bloodshed were over.

Within an hour of the signing of the armistice in Korea, President Eisenhower gave official notification to the American people that the war was finally over. Here is the president's live, televised address in its entirely.

Source: *Public Papers of the Presidents of the United States, Dwight D. Eisenhower, 1953* (Washington, D.C.: U.S. Government Printing Office, 1960), pp. 520-522.

My fellow citizens:

Tonight we greet, with prayers of thanksgiving, the official news that an armistice was signed almost an hour ago in

Korea. It will quickly bring to an end the fighting between the United Nations forces and the Communist armies. For this Nation the cost of repelling aggression has been high. In thousands of homes it has been incalculable. It has been paid in terms of tragedy.

With special feelings of sorrow — and of solemn gratitude — we think of those who were called upon to lay down their lives in that far-off land to prove once again that only courage and sacrifice can keep freedom alive upon the earth. To the widows and orphans of this war, and to those veterans who bear disabling wounds, America renews tonight her pledge of lasting devotion and care.

Our thoughts turn also to those other Americans wearied by many months of imprisonment behind the enemy lines. The swift return of all of them will bring joy to thousands of families. It will be evidence of good faith on the part of those with whom we have signed this armistice.

Soldiers, sailors, and airmen of 16 different countries have stood as partners beside us throughout these long and bitter months. America's thanks go to each. In this struggle we have seen the United Nations meet the challenge of aggression — not with pathetic words of protest, but with deeds of decisive purpose. It is proper that we salute particularly the valorous armies of the Republic of Korea, for they have done even more than prove their right to freedom. Inspired by President Syngman Rhee, they have given an example of courage and patriotism which again demonstrates that men of the West and men of the East can fight and work and live together side by side in pursuit of a just and noble cause.

And so at long last the carnage of war is to cease and the negotiations of the conference table [are] to begin. On this Sabbath evening each of us devoutly prays that all nations may come to see the wisdom of composing differences in this fashion before, rather than after, there is resort to brutal and futile battle.

Now as we strive to bring about that wisdom, there is, in this moment of sober satisfaction, one thought that must discipline our emotions and steady our resolution. It is this: we have won an armistice on a single battleground — not peace in the world. We may not now relax our guard nor cease our quest.

Throughout the coming months, during the period of prisoner screening and exchange, and during the possibly longer period of the political conference which looks toward the unification of Korea, we and our United Nations Allies must be vigilant against the possibility of untoward developments.

And as we do so, we shall fervently strive to insure that this armistice will, in fact, bring free peoples one step nearer to their goals of a world at peace.

My friends, almost 90 years ago, Abraham Lincoln at the end of a war delivered his second Inaugural Address. At the end of that speech he spoke some words that I think more nearly express the true feelings of America tonight than would any other words ever spoken or written. You will recall them:

"With malice toward none; with charity for all; with firmness in the right as God gives us to see the right, let us strive on to finish the work we are in...to do all which may achieve and cherish a just and a lasting peace, among ourselves, and with all nations."

This is our resolve and our dedication.

Suggested Further Reading

In addition to the readings included in the text, the following studies are also useful.

Blair, Clay. *The Forgotten War: America in Korea, 1950-1953*. New York: Times Books, 1987.

Cumings, Bruce. *The Origins of the Korean War*, 2 vols. Princeton: Princeton University Press, 1981-1990.

Foot, Rosemary. *The Wrong War: American Policy and the Dimensions of the Korean Conflict, 1950-1953*. Ithaca: Cornell University Press, 1985.

James, D. Clayton. *Refighting the Last War: Command and Crisis in Korea, 1950-1953*. New York: The Free Press, 1993.

Kaufman, Burton I. *The Korean War: Challenges in Crisis, Credibility, and Command*. New York: McGraw-Hill, 1997.

MacDonald, Callum A. *Korea*. New York: The Free Press, 1987.

Rees, David. *Korea: The Limited War*. London: Macmillan, 1964.

Spanier, John. *The Truman-MacArthur Controversy and the Korean War*. New York: Norton, 1965.

Toland, John. *In Mortal Combat: Korea, 1950-1953*. New York: William Morrow, 1991.

Whelan, Richard. *Drawing the Line: The Korean War, 1950-1953*. Boston: Little, Brown, 1990.

About the Editor

Karl E. Valois has served as chairman of the Social Studies Department at St. Joseph High School in Trumball, Connecticut and has taught at the University of Connecticut. He as been awarded fellowships at Yale University and the University of Connecticut, where he also received a Ph.D. in history.

Karl has appeared on radio and television, helped to edit several books on American and European history, and has published over two dozen articles.